■ BRITISH HISTORY MAKERS
WINSTON CHURCHILL

LEON ASHWORTH

CHERRYTREE BOOKS

A Cherrytree Book

Designed and produced by
A S Publishing

Copyright © this edition
Evans Brothers Ltd 2005
Published 2000 by
Cherrytree Press a
division of Evans Brothers
Ltd, 2A Portman Mansions
Chiltern St, London W1U 6NR

British Library Cataloguing in Publication Data

Ashworth, Leon
    Winston Churchill. – (British history makers)
    1.Churchill, Winston S. (Winston Spencer), 1874-1965
    2.Prime ministers – Great Britain
    3.Great Britain – Politics and government – 1901-1936
    4.Great Britain Politics and government – 1936-1945
    5.Great Britain – History – 20th century
    I.Title
    941'.082'092

ISBN 1 84234 282 7

First published 2002

Printed and bound in Hong Kong by Wing King Tong Co. Ltd

Acknowledgments
Design: Richard Rowan
Editorial: John Collins
Artwork: Malcolm Porter
Consultant: Brian Williams
Photographs: *AKG London* 3 left (& 15 top left), 12 bottom
left, 17 right, 21 top, 23 bottom; *The Art Archive* 11
bottom, 13 bottom, 14/15 bottom, 23 left centre; *Britain
on View* 6 bottom, 16 bottom; *FDR Library* Back cover
(& 24/25 top); *Hulton Getty* 1 (& 28 bottom), 4, 7
bottom, 8, 9 left top & bottom, 10 right centre, 11
right top, 12 right top & bottom, 13 top, 14 left,
14/15 background, 15 top right, 18 bottom left,
18/19 bottom, 19 bottom right, 20/21 top &
background, 21 right, 22 top, 22/23 background, 23 top,
24/25 background & centre, 25 top, 26, 27, 29; *Imperial War
Museum* 2 left bottom (& 25 bottom) & right top (& 21
bottom), 3 bottom (& 22 bottom), 24 bottom; *Mary Evans
Picture Library* Front cover bottom (& 20 bottom), 2 right bottom (& 16 top), 3
right (& 19 top), 7 left, 9 top right, 10/11 top, 14 right centre, 15 centre, 17 top,
18 top; *National Portrait Gallery* 6 top & centre; *"P A" News Photo Library* Front
cover portrait, 2 left top (& 16 centre); *Sandhurst Military Academy* 10 bottom;
Winston Churchill Memorial and Library, Westminster College, Missouri 5.

CONTENTS

■ THE GREAT COMMONER ■

W INSTON CHURCHILL was praised in his lifetime as 'the greatest living Englishman', although he was half-American. He was also called 'the Great Commoner', because he served as an MP (Member of Parliament) in the House of Commons for over 60 years. From a family of dukes, he remained plain Mr Winston Churchill for most of his life, accepting a knighthood only as an old man, so that he died Sir Winston Churchill.

Churchill led Britain as prime minister during the darkest years of World War II (1939-45). He was an inspiring war leader, and people came to know and love his growling voice on the radio, promising victory even when the war was going badly. They got used to seeing pictures of Churchill, in newspapers and on film, visiting battlefields and walking over the rubble of bombed cities, often with a cigar in his mouth and his hand raised in the 'V for Victory' sign.

Churchill had a long life, much of it spent in politics. The son of a politician, he felt it was his destiny to serve his country. He was a distinguished writer, a keen amateur painter, a stirring speaker. Above all, he was a person who loved his country, its language and its history, and when its need was greatest, spent all his energies in its defence.

CHURCHILL'S LIFE

1874 Churchill born.
1899 Prisoner of war in South Africa.
1900 Elected to Parliament.
1908 Marries Clementine Hozier.
1914-18 World War I.
1939-45 World War II.
1940 Becomes prime minister.
1945 Loses general election.
1951-55 Prime minister again.
1964 Retires from House of Commons.
1965 Churchill dies.

▲ Churchill's famous wartime 'V for Victory' salute.

▼ Churchill's signature – the S stood for Spencer.

■ BORN IN A PALACE ■

WINSTON LEONARD Spencer Churchill was born on 30 November 1874. He first opened his eyes in one of the many rooms of a vast mansion, Blenheim Palace, in Oxfordshire, England. The house had been built in the 1700s for his famous ancestor, John Churchill, first Duke of Marlborough (1650-1722).

BRILLIANT PARENTS

Winston's father, Lord Randolph Churchill, was a newly elected MP and one of the rising stars of British politics. He was clever and witty, and his friends saw him as a future prime minister. Randolph and his wife shone in London society. She was a beautiful and wealthy American, Jeanette (Jennie) Jerome. Winston was their first child. His birth at Blenheim was accidental. His mother was visiting the family home, and when the baby arrived sooner than expected, he had to be dressed in borrowed clothes.

EVENTS

1874 Winston Churchill born in November. Lawn tennis is played for the first time in England.
1875 Captain Matthew Webb becomes the first man to swim the English Channel.
1876 In the United States, General Custer and his 7th Cavalry are killed at the Battle of the Little Big Horn. Queen Victoria becomes empress of India. Alexander Graham Bell invents the telephone.
1879 Thomas Edison shows off his new electric light bulb.
1880 Australia's most notorious outlaw, Ned Kelly, is captured, tried and hanged.

▲ Winston's father, Lord Randolph Churchill. His wife, Jennie Jerome, was a New Yorker and the couple married against their parents' wishes.

▼ Blenheim Palace was a gift from Queen Anne and a grateful nation to the great soldier, John Churchill (right).

BRINGING UP BABY

IN THE Victorian world into which Winston was born, large families were common, but many small children died. Childhood diseases, such as scarlet fever and diphtheria, were feared as killers. Working mothers relied on their older children to help care for babies. Only better-off parents could afford paid help – servants to do the housework, and a nanny (below) to look after the children until they were sent to school.

A LONELY CHILDHOOD

Neither of Winston's busy parents spent much time with their baby son. He was well cared for by nurses, but was often lonely, missing his mother and father. In 1877 the family moved from London to Ireland, where Winston's grandfather, the Duke of Marlborough, represented Queen Victoria as viceroy. Winston now had a favourite nurse, who became almost a second mother, his nanny Mrs Everest. He adored her and called her 'Woomany'. She took him to watch the soldiers parading in Dublin, and later they enjoyed summer holidays together, at the seaside.

In 1880 Winston peered into the cradle to admire his new baby brother, Jack. The Churchills then returned to London, where Lord Randolph continued his political career. Little Winston faced two problems: stopping baby Jack from breaking his toy soldiers, and going to school.

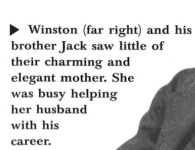

▶ Winston (far right) and his brother Jack saw little of their charming and elegant mother. She was busy helping her husband with his career.

■ A TROUBLESOME BOY ■

WINSTON LOVED reading, especially adventure stories like *Treasure Island*, but he hated his first school. It was a small private boarding school for boys in Ascot. The teachers beat the pupils for bad work and bad behaviour, and gave them too little to eat. How Winston longed to be with his mother, at a London party, eating all the treats at the buffet table!

At school, Winston's favourite subjects were history and geography. He loved to gaze at the world map, on which the British Empire was marked in red. He wondered if he would ever see any of these faraway places. He liked drawing, too, but his handwriting was an untidy scrawl.

CHANGE FOR THE BETTER
In 1884 Winston's parents sent him to a new school at Hove, on the south coast. Here Winston was much happier. The two lady teachers were kind and his schoolwork improved. He was able to swim in the sea, and ride horses – a sport he loved more than any other.

LIFE'S UPS AND DOWNS
By now Lord Randolph was high on the political ladder. In 1886 he was made Chancellor of the Exchequer, in charge of the country's finances. But soon he made a bad mistake. He resigned over a small matter, thinking

EVENTS

1881 United States President Garfield dies after being shot.
1882 Karl Marx, German founder of Communism, dies in London.
1885 Karl Benz drives the world's first car. At a conference, 15 European nations agree to 'carve up' much of Africa. Britain's General Gordon is killed in Khartoum, Sudan.
1886 First railway across Canada is completed. Churchill's father resigns from the government.
1887 Queen Victoria celebrates her Golden Jubilee.
1888 Winston starts at Harrow School. English soccer clubs start the first professional league.
1889 Eiffel Tower is built in Paris.

FIFTY YEARS A QUEEN

QUEEN Victoria became Britain's queen in 1837, at the age of 18. In 1887 she celebrated 50 years on the throne. For the service of thanksgiving in Westminster Abbey, the queen (still mourning her dead husband Albert, who died in 1861) refused to wear a crown. Instead she chose a bonnet of white lace trimmed with diamonds. Winston joined his family in London to watch the Jubilee parade, cheering as

▲ As a boy, Winston lacked confidence. He stammered when he spoke and did poorly at school.

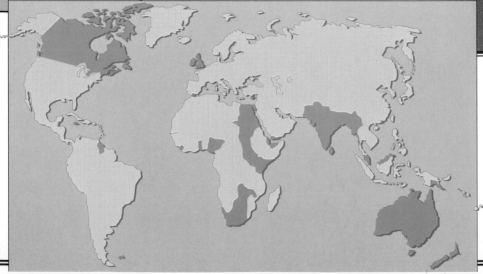

◄ The British Empire in 1887. The empire brought Britain wealth and power but Churchill realised that the colonies must sooner or later have their independence.

troops from all over the British Empire marched through the capital.

▲ **Boys in their summer uniform at Harrow School. Winston had been at the school for 18 months before his father came to visit.**

▶ **Winston shows off his school uniform. His parents thought Harrow would be good for his health because it was on a hill, unlike his father's school, Eton, which was in a valley.**

that he was sure to be invited back into the government before long. But he wasn't. To add to the family's troubles, Winston caught pneumonia. He was seriously ill, and nearly died.

The celebrations for Queen Victoria's Jubilee in 1887 were overshadowed by Winston's gloom at facing exams to enter Harrow, a famous public school. Although the Latin exam baffled him – he left the paper blank, save for his name – Winston passed and in 1888 he began his new school.

He impressed his teachers with his essay-writing, and his ability to learn and recite long poems, but was often in trouble for being late, losing books, and forgetting what he was told.

■ THE YOUNG SOLDIER ■

WINSTON'S PARENTS decided that the army would suit their harum-scarum son. He twice failed the exam to enter Sandhurst military academy for officers, and was sent for private lessons. Eventually, in 1893, he scraped into the college, but not without a terrible telling-off by letter from his father. Lord Randolph was a shadow of his old self. His health was failing fast and he had money worries. There was no money to buy Winston a horse, and even worse, the Churchills sacked Winston's nanny, Mrs Everest.

▼ The Royal Military Academy Sandhurst where Churchill, seen (left) with two fellow cadets, learned his military leadership skills.

GETTING AWAY FROM SADNESS

Winston enjoyed the life of a soldier at Sandhurst. He came 20th out of a class of 130, and was determined to join the cavalry. Christmas 1894 was a time of sorrow. A world cruise had failed to restore Lord Randolph's health, and he was clearly a dying man. The end came on 24 January 1895. That summer, Mrs Everest also died.

After these sad events, Winston needed a change, and he travelled to the United States. While there, he managed to arrange a trip to Cuba, where a revolution was taking place. This was a profitable adventure, for he earned money writing reports from Cuba for a London newspaper.

GETTING WHAT HE WANTED

Winston returned home to join a cavalry regiment, the 4th Hussars. In 1896 the young Lieutenant Churchill sailed with the Hussars and their

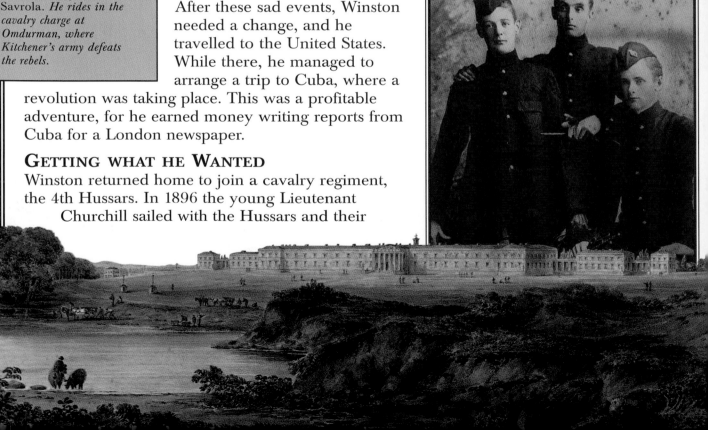

SOLDIERS OF THE QUEEN

WHILE the Royal Navy ruled the waves, the less glamorous British army – the 'thin red line' – defended the empire. When Churchill joined the army as a young cavalry officer, he was seeking adventure, travel and the chance to make his name. Poorer men – English, Welsh, Scots and Irish – joined the army for regular pay and three meals a day. Seeing the world came with the job.

▼ The battle of Omdurman where Churchill took part in a cavalry charge. The charge contributed little to the British victory but gave young Winston a thrill.

horses to India. There he joined a military expedition to the wild North-West Frontier, and wrote a book about this adventure. Back home, he made his first public speech, in support of the Conservative Party. He was 23.

Winston had learned the importance of asking powerful people for help in getting what he wanted. Seeking more action, he wrote to the prime minister, Lord Salisbury, and was soon in a steamship with the 21st Lancers, on his way to Africa. In the Sudan, Egyptian and British soldiers were fighting rebels. General Gordon, a national hero, had been killed there in 1885, and now General Kitchener was out for revenge. At the battle of Omdurman in 1898, Churchill rode with the Lancers in the British army's last great cavalry charge – 'the most dangerous two minutes I shall live to see'.

▲ Churchill as a lieutenant in the 4th (Queen's Own) Hussars in 1896. His visit to India gave him a lifelong love of the sub-continent.

■ WAR HERO ■

HOME FROM the Sudan, Churchill decided to try his luck in politics. He was already well known in London, where his mother had many friends, among them politicians Herbert Asquith and Arthur Balfour, both of whom went on to be prime minister.

EVENTS

1899 *Start of the Boer War. Churchill goes to South Africa as a reporter. His mother works on a hospital ship, treating the wounded.*

1901 *Queen Victoria dies. Edward VII becomes king. Marconi sends the first radio signals across the Atlantic. Theodore Roosevelt becomes US president after President McKinley is shot dead.*

1903 *Wright brothers fly the first aeroplane. Marie Curie wins a Nobel Prize, for discovering radium.*

1906 *Liberal Party wins the British general election. San Francisco is reduced to rubble by an earthquake. Britain launches the first modern battleship, HMS Dreadnought.*

1908 *Mr and Mrs Churchill begin married life.*

ADVENTURE IN SOUTH AFRICA

Churchill resigned as an army officer and in 1899 stood for election as MP for Oldham in Lancashire, where he was soundly defeated. He needed a job, and was hired as a war correspondent for the *Morning Post* newspaper, which sent him to South Africa to cover the Boer War.

In South Africa, Churchill was soon making news rather than reporting it. Helping to rescue a British train ambushed by Boer guerrillas, he was taken prisoner and locked up in a school. He escaped through a lavatory window and was smuggled out of danger on a train. He enjoyed Christmas 1899 in Durban and sailed for Britain as a war hero to campaign in the 1900 general election. This time the voters of

▼ **Helping to rescue a British train ambushed by Boer guerrillas, young Winston was taken prisoner and locked up in a school.**

▲ **Watched by a vulture, Churchill hides from a passing Boer patrol. The Boers offered £25 for his recapture dead or alive.**

Oldham flocked to his cause, and he was elected their MP.

MONEY, A MINISTER AND MARRIAGE

Money remained a problem, since at the time MPs were not paid. To earn some money, he made lecture tours in Britain and America, describing his South African adventure. In Parliament, he learned his way around the corridors of power. He also wrote a biography of his father. In 1904 he upset his Conservative Party friends by deserting them to join the rival Liberals. Two years later he was a minister in the new Liberal government.

Changing sides cost Churchill some friends, though many people still found the young man's self-confidence and enthusiasm refreshing. Among those he won over was Clementine Hozier, whom Winston married in 1908. It was the start of a long and happy partnership.

▲ Winston and Clementine, photographed the week before their wedding. They were to have five children and 'lived happily ever after'.

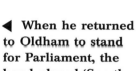

◀ When he returned to Oldham to stand for Parliament, the band played 'See the Conquering Hero Comes', and Churchill was elected.

SOUTH AFRICAN WAR

THE Boer War (1899-1902) was a struggle in South Africa between the British and Dutch-speaking settlers, known as Boers. The trouble began in the 1870s. The Boer farmers wanted to rule themselves and not be part of the British Empire. At first, their guerrilla fighters outfoxed the British army, attacking on horseback in small groups called commandos. They were eventually defeated, and in 1910 Boer and British colonies were united in the Union of South Africa.

■ MINISTER AT WAR ■

CHURCHILL'S RISE was rapid. In 1908, Prime Minister Asquith made him President of the Board of Trade. He lost the by-election (which new ministers then had to undergo), but was voted back as MP for Dundee. He won a reputation as a reformer, bringing in laws to limit miners' working hours. But in a new and more important job as Home Secretary, he showed a sterner side to his character by calling out the army to scatter striking Welsh miners. Like his father, he wanted to see a solution to the problems in Ireland, and supported moves to give the Irish self-government (though these moves failed).

EVENTS

1910 Edward VII dies of pneumonia. His son George V becomes king.
1912 Norwegian explorer Roald Amundsen reaches the South Pole. The liner Titanic is lost at sea.
1914 Start of World War I, a war that brings trench misery, poison gas, and aeroplanes and tanks in battle.
1915 Churchill's plan to attack Turkey in the Dardanelles fails.
1916 Battle of the Somme; more than one million men are wounded or killed.
1917 Churchill back in government. Russian Revolution overthrows the Tsar. Civil war in Russia follows.
1918 World War I ends; Britain alone has lost nearly 800,000 men dead.

▶ **Churchill saw Germany's military build-up at first hand when he was invited by Kaiser Wilhelm II to view German military exercises not long before the war began.**

REVOLUTION IN RUSSIA

CHURCHILL was horrified by events in Russia, where in October 1917 the Bolsheviks, led by Vladimir Ilich Lenin (right), seized power and set up a Communist government. The Tsar (emperor) and his family were arrested and later murdered. In the civil war that followed, Churchill urged the British government to do all it could to help defeat the Communists. Churchill remained staunchly anti-Communist all his life.

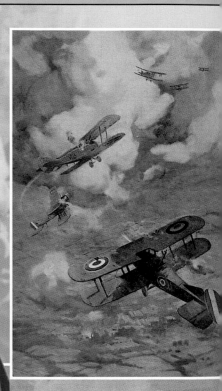

14

▼ World War I was mostly fought by infantry in trenches, but also in the air (left), for the first time, and at sea (below). The development of the tank, (bottom) and the arrival of the Americans brought to an end a war that had cost the lives of millions.

RULER OF THE KING'S NAVY

▲ Churchill acknowledged the importance of women workers during the war. Here he visits a shipyard to cheer on their vital efforts.

In 1911 Churchill was moved to the Admiralty, in charge of the navy. This was a job he relished. He had stood beside Germany's emperor watching army manoeuvres, and was sure that war would come, sooner or later. He saw to it that the Royal Navy had more modern ships than the German Navy. When war began in 1914, the British fleet was ready.

As a war minister, Churchill was energetic and determined. He went to Belgium to organize the defence of Antwerp (even though this was a job for a general, not a minister). His ambitious scheme to attack the Turks in the Dardanelles (1915), however, ground to a disastrous halt on the beaches of Gallipoli. Thousands of British, Australian and New Zealand troops died, and Churchill resigned. He went to France, to serve with the Royal Scots regiment, but was soon back in Parliament to speak out against the bad generalship that had cost so many soldiers' lives during the battle of the Somme in 1916.

END OF THE GREAT WAR

Churchill was a friend of the Welsh politician David Lloyd George, his equal as a brilliant speech-maker. Lloyd George formed a new government in 1917 and invited Churchill to join it, as minister for munitions (weapons). He helped launch a formidable new weapon, the tank, which together with the arrival of American troops in 1917 brought an end to the 'war to end wars'.

In Russia, the Communist Revolution of 1917 was followed by civil war. Although Churchill sent help to the 'White Russians' fighting the Communist 'Reds', their cause was hopeless.

■ THE CHANCE HAS GONE ■

PEACE RETURNED to a Britain weakened by the cost of the war. Peacetime politics returned with the 1922 election, which Churchill fought from a wheelchair while recovering from appendicitis. He lost. He was, he said ruefully, 'without an office, without a seat, without a party and without an appendix'. To cheer himself up, and earn money to support his wife and children, he wrote *The World Crisis*, a history of the war, and with the money bought Chartwell, a country house in Kent which became the Churchill family home.

IN FROM THE COLD

Churchill was desperate to return to Parliament, but having turned his back on the Liberal Party, was defeated twice in elections (1923, 1924). He had become an outsider, without official party backing. It was a case of 'third time

► This caricature of 1919 is simply labelled 'Winnie', the pet name by which he was known.

▲ The Churchills' two eldest children, Diana and Randolph (centre) with their cousin Johnny, Jack Churchill's son.

◄ Chartwell was always a place of happiness for Churchill. 'A day from Chartwell is a day wasted', he said.

◄Millions of workers lost their jobs following the General Strike and during the trade slump that began in 1929. Britain stayed largely peaceful but there was some street fighting. Here the police break up a workers' demonstration.

HER ZU UNS!

Hinein in die Hitler-Jugend

lucky' when towards the end of 1924 he was elected MP for Epping, in Essex, as an independent 'constitutionalist'. The new prime minister, Stanley Baldwin, invited him to return to the Conservative Party, and offered him a job – a big job. To everyone's surprise, Winston Churchill became Chancellor of the Exchequer.

AND OUT AGAIN

At the time, the whole world had economic problems, and Churchill was not good at financial affairs. Unemployment rose, and in 1926 Britain was paralysed by its first and only General Strike. Churchill saw in this workers' protest a threat of Communist revolution. The government fell in 1929, and left Churchill 'in the wilderness'. A new national coalition government, formed in 1931 by Conservative and Labour leaders, could find no room for him.

During the 1930s, Churchill watched events in Europe with alarm, particularly the rise of Adolf Hitler and his Nazis in Germany. He warned of a new war, and in speeches and newspaper articles urged Britain to modernise its army and navy, and build new planes for its air force. But he was almost a lone voice, to which few people listened.

THE RISE OF THE NAZIS

GERMANY was ruined by its defeat in World War I, and the peace terms it was forced to sign. Its money became worthless, and by 1932 six million Germans had no jobs. A former soldier named Adolf Hitler, leader of the Nazi Party, swept to power on a tide of discontent. Hitler became Chancellor (chief minister) in 1933. Young people were encouraged to join the 'Hitler Youth'. The Nazis stamped out opposition, preached race hate against Jews and 'inferior' peoples, and boasted that they would conquer a new German Reich (empire).

■ SLIDE TOWARDS WAR ■

AS EUROPE SLID towards a second world war, Churchill kept busy with his writing. *My Early Life* was a lively story of his own youthful adventures, and he produced a long history of his famous ancestor, the Duke of Marlborough. His mind was full of the threat from Germany. Churchill knew only too well 'what vile and wicked folly' war was, but he continued to speak out, even when those calling for peace accused him of being a warmonger.

BRITAIN LOSES A KING

Winston still had some friends in high places. One was the Prince of Wales. When King George V died in 1935, the prince became Edward VIII. He was in love with an American, Wallis Simpson, who had been divorced. The new king, charming but weak, insisted that she must be his queen. When his mother, his family and the government said

LIFE IN THE 1930S

EUROPE and America recovered during the 1930s from the slump in trade and business of 1929-30. In Britain, where many people had been out of work, life got better slowly. New housing estates were built, and there were more cars on the roads, for ordinary people as well as the military. For entertainment, people could enjoy a film at the cinema, or dance to a live band at the local dance hall. At home, families listened to the wireless (radio). Television broadcasts began in 1936, but few people owned television sets.

◀ **Edward VIII and Mrs Simpson. Despite Churchill's full support, the new king abdicated and went into exile as Duke of Windsor.**

▶ **Churchill bitterly opposed Neville Chamberlain, calling his triumphant 'peace for our time' a 'total and unmitigated defeat'.**

no, he gave up the throne and went into exile abroad. Had Churchill backed another loser?

WAR CLOUDS GATHER

Another friend was the foreign secretary Anthony Eden, but when Eden resigned in 1938 in protest at the government's 'appeasement' of Germany, Churchill felt 'the dark waters of despair' closing over him. He declared that the Munich 'peace agreement' between prime minister Neville Chamberlain and the German dictator Hitler was a calamity. The paper Chamberlain brought home was worthless, though Britain did gain a year to prepare its defences, for everyone now saw the clouds of war gathering.

On 3 September 1939, Britain and France declared war on Germany, which had invaded their ally, Poland. Churchill had mixed feelings: sorrow that his worst fears were realised and relief that he might once more play a part in great affairs. As Britain went to war, he was asked to return to the Admiralty, once again to order the Royal Navy into battle. He tore into action, despatching orders and letters in all directions. But after months of little real fighting, the Navy's first major campaign, in Norway, ended in withdrawal. By April 1940, the British people had learned a lesson; the six-month 'phoney' war was over; the real battle was about to begin.

▲ Hitler's Nazi rallies and propaganda brought his party to power in 1933. He swiftly became dictator and set about destroying all opposition and conquering Europe.

▼ Some people in Britain admired the way Hitler had restored the German nation, but Churchill saw the danger. His warnings fell on deaf ears, but people remembered when he was proved right.

■ BATTLING FOR BRITAIN ■

THE WAR was going badly, with defeat following defeat. In May 1940 German troops swept through Belgium and Holland into France. On 10 May Neville Chamberlain resigned as prime minister. The king told him that Churchill was the best choice to take over, and Churchill became prime minister, taking personal charge of Britain's defences.

On 13 May he spoke to the House of Commons, promising that Britain would fight on sea, land and air 'with all the strength that God can give us'. Even if Britain fell, the Commonwealth and Empire would fight on, and the United States would rally to the defence of freedom.

RETREAT AND RECOVERY

British and Allied troops were caught up in the confusion of France's defeat, and fell back to the coast at the port of Dunkirk. From the beaches there, over

▲ **Churchill inspects a gallant naval crew, who were rescued after their ship was wrecked in enemy waters.**

▼ **Thousands of troops, stranded under bombardment at Dunkirk in France, were rescued by small ships that ferried them back across the Channel to England.**

300,000 soldiers were rescued by a flotilla of small boats and brought to England. To keep France in the war, Churchill even offered a union with Britain, but on 14 June France surrendered. Britain stood alone. Churchill knew that the British people must brace themselves for what he called 'their finest hour'.

▲ German and Italian bombers attacked British towns. Londoners endured the Blitz, along with the king and queen, seen (below) visiting a bomb site with Churchill.

WAR IN THE AIR

The German air force began attacking airfields in southern England. They aimed to clear the skies of British planes before invading Britain by sea. Their planes were met by the fighters of the Royal Air Force, and all through the summer people watched as the Battle of Britain raged above their towns and villages. Meeting such strong resistance, the Germans changed their plans, and began bombing British cities. This was the start of the Blitz.

Churchill rallied everyone to the country's defence, from the local volunteers or Home Guard ('Dad's Army') to the young pilots of the Royal Air Force; from families in air raid shelters to workers in factories. The prime minister pinned his long-term hopes on the United States. Only its strength and riches could speedily save the free world from sinking into a 'New Dark Age'.

FIGHTING BACK

A tireless worker, Churchill often appeared on the bombed streets wearing a 'siren suit' (overalls) and tin hat. He spent many nights on a camp bed in the underground War Room in bomb-battered London. His mind was full of schemes for fighting back, for turning the tide of defeat into a wave of victory.

DESERVE VICTORY!

RALLYING THE PEOPLE

PEOPLE followed the war news in the newspapers and on the radio. Churchill's superb speeches rallied people at home and abroad, in the darkest times, when defeat looked possible. He never thought of giving up, even if the country was invaded. He told the British people: 'We shall fight on the beaches, we shall fight on the landing grounds, we shall fight in the fields and in the streets, we shall fight in the hills; we shall never surrender'.

■ ALLIES AT WAR ■

CHURCHILL SET out the aims of the war starkly. Hitler was the enemy, and anyone who joined the fight against Hitler was a friend. Having given up any hopes of invading Britain, Hitler turned his eyes to the east. In 1941 German armies invaded Russia. Churchill at once offered help to the Russian leader Josef Stalin, a dictator whom he privately disliked and distrusted.

FRIENDS ACROSS THE OCEAN

Being half-American himself, Churchill naturally looked across the Atlantic Ocean for his most important ally. Many Americans wanted no part in a European war, though President Roosevelt was friendly and sent regular messages to Churchill. In December 1941 the Japanese navy attacked the United States base of Pearl Harbor in Hawaii, and the Americans entered the war against Japan and Japan's ally, Germany. Churchill was relieved. Pearl Harbor was a disaster, but with the United States in the war, Churchill wrote that 'there was no more doubt about the end'.

THE TIDE TURNS

In 1942 the Japanese captured the Philippines, Malaya and the British naval base of Singapore. Despite these setbacks,

EVENTS

1941 *German armies invade Russia. Japan bombs US Navy ships in Pearl Harbor, bringing the USA into the war.*
1942 *Japanese conquer southeast Asia. Battle of El Alamein begins Allied recovery in North Africa. Churchill goes to Russia to meet Stalin.*
1943 *Germans surrender at siege of Stalingrad in Russia. Allied forces cross from North Africa to invade southern Italy. Italy surrenders. Churchill, Roosevelt and Stalin meet.*

▲ Workers in bomb-blasted Manchester cheer Churchill. As war leader, he was inspired by the British people's endurance of the German onslaught.

▼ Churchill and Roosevelt (seated left), seen here with Canada's prime minister and governor general, met several times to discuss future tactics.

TOTAL WAR

THE Germans used air power to support tanks on the ground during their attacks on France and Russia. The Royal Air Force saved Britain in 1940. Japanese planes launched from aircraft carriers raided Pearl Harbor (right) in 1941, and the biggest naval battles of the Pacific war were fought between carrier air fleets. British cities were attacked by German bombers from 1940, and by 1942 British and American bombers in huge numbers (1000 planes in a night) were hitting back at targets in Germany and occupied Europe.

▼ The Germans met ferocious Russian resistance at Stalingrad. After five months of freezing weather and shortage of supplies, they surrendered.

the tide was starting to turn. The Russians were fighting back, aided by the freezing cold of the Russian winter. In the desert of North Africa, British and Commonwealth armies, at first driven back almost into Egypt by the Germans, recovered to win the battle of El Alamein. American guns, ships, planes and troops crossed the Atlantic in growing numbers. By the middle of 1943 the Allies were on the attack, and Churchill directed his energy into keeping the alliance together.

BALANCE OF POWER

In 1943 the 'Big Three' leaders – Churchill, Roosevelt and Stalin – met for the first time at Teheran in Persia (Iran). They discussed plans for an Allied invasion of western Europe. Now Churchill began to realise that of the Big Three, his was the weakest voice. Russia controlled events in eastern Europe; America the war in Asia against Japan. When the war was won, the new world order would be different from the old.

▼ A German tank crew views smoking British tanks in North Africa. By May 1943 Germany and Italy were beaten in the desert.

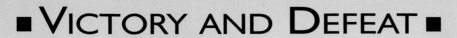

■ VICTORY AND DEFEAT ■

I N JUNE 1944 the Allied invasion of France began. Commanded by United States general Dwight Eisenhower, a million men crossed the English Channel to free France and its neighbours. Churchill was desperate to be there, and would have sailed in a naval cruiser, had not the king ordered him to stay at home. Impatiently, the prime minister waited for news that the landings had been a success. As the German armies fell back before the Allied advance, French people welcomed Allied troops with tears and cheers. It was the beginning of the end of the war.

PROBLEMS OF POWER

The Big Three met at Yalta in the Crimea (USSR) in February 1945. With German defences crumbling, Churchill watched Stalin's armies advancing across eastern Europe. Fearing the spread of Communist dictatorship, he wanted the Allied armies to race for Berlin and finish the war in Europe quickly. He foresaw an 'iron curtain' falling across Europe, dividing free peoples from peoples enslaved by tyranny. But in April 1945 his old friend President Roosevelt died suddenly. Vice-president Harry S Truman took over, and

◀ Churchill, Roosevelt and Stalin met at Yalta, on the Black Sea, to discuss the future of Europe. Roosevelt was readier than Churchill to let Stalin have his way.

America turned its attention to ending the war in the Pacific. Churchill's power to control events was shrinking.

CHEERS AND FAREWELL

In May 1945 crowds danced in streets around the world to celebrate VE Day, the end of the war in Europe. In London, Churchill joined the royal family on the balcony of Buckingham Palace. He was cheered by all.

Yet within a month, he was prime minister no longer. A general election was held in June 1945. Churchill was still cheered as he travelled round the country, yet when the votes were counted, the result was victory for the Labour Party and their programme of social reforms. Churchill had won the war, but lost the peace.

PEACE AND REFLECTION

The Churchills moved out of 10 Downing Street, the prime minister's official London home, and in moved Labour's leader, Clement Attlee. It was Attlee, not Churchill, who flew off to the new Big Three meeting in Potsdam, Germany. Two atomic bombs ended the war with Japan in August 1945. By then Winston Churchill, MP for Woodford in Essex, was left with his wartime papers, to look back on five historic years.

▲ The atomic bomb dropped on Nagasaki, Japan, in 1945, ended the war.

▲ People danced in the streets on VE Day and Londoners flocked to Buckingham Palace to cheer Churchill and the royal family.

◀ Together with General Montgomery (right), Churchill surveys the devastated French town of Caen, the scene of fierce fighting during the liberation of France.

THE PEOPLE'S WAR

WORLD War II affected everyone in Britain. Many families lost their homes in bombing raids. Children were evacuated from the cities to the countryside. Millions of men left their homes to join the forces. Women, including Princess (later Queen) Elizabeth, joined up too, as truck drivers, factory workers, or 'land army girls', helping on the farms. Food was rationed but most people made the best of things, often grumbling about shortages (one egg a week, no sugar, no bananas), but on the whole staying cheerful – and surprisingly healthy.

25

■ VOICE FOR FREEDOM ■

CHURCHILL WAS still leader of the Conservative Party. For the next six years he spoke out against government policies his party opposed, such as the nationalisation of the railways and coal mines. He was most interested in world affairs, and was saddened by the break-up of the British Empire, which started with India's independence in 1947. He accepted that the Indian people, like others in the empire, would sooner or later run their own affairs.

RESHAPING THE WORLD
A new world was emerging from the ruins of the war, which Churchill wrote about in his history of *The Second World War*. Anxious for the future, he believed the new United Nations Organization must be supported, to prevent further wars. In a memorable speech at Fulton, Missouri, he urged Britain and America to work together to defend freedom against the threat of Communism.

▲ Churchill, wearing a ceremonial uniform, inspects a guard of honour at Dover Castle in 1946.

▲ With the war over, Churchill had more time to spend with his family. Here he attends the christening of a granddaughter.

▼ Elizabeth II's coronation in 1953. Having refused a peerage, Churchill was persuaded by the new young queen to accept a knighthood.

BRITAIN IN THE 1950S

IN THE 1950s the British people enjoyed a new prosperity. Rationing came to an end, and there was more to buy in the shops. More people could afford cars, refrigerators and washing machines. Television was taking over from the wireless and the cinema. Britain could make marvels of technology, such as the new Comet jet airliner, but still had steam trains and coal fires. Germany and Japan, rebuilt from the ruin of defeat, were fast becoming modern industrial giants.

▼ Having led Britain through its darkest days, Churchill was rejected by voters in 1945. Instead of retiring, he led the Opposition and was returned to power in 1951. Though old, ill and tired, he still had enough fighting spirit to give the old Victory sign.

America and Russia, former allies, were now practically enemies, and both were developing terrifying new atomic weapons and missiles. The Cold War had begun. Churchill supported the new North Atlantic Treaty Organization (NATO) to defend the West, and also backed moves to create a European Common Market, which later grew into the European Union.

BACK IN POWER

In the 1950 general election, Churchill led the Conservatives with zest and almost pulled off victory. Weakened by the war, Britain was no longer a front-rank world power, and the British people were tired of shortages and rationing. In a second election, in 1951, they voted Labour out, and Churchill in. At the age of 76, he was prime minister again, with his wartime colleague Anthony Eden as foreign secretary.

AND RESIGNATION

In 1953 the ageing prime minister relished the pomp and ceremony of the coronation of the young queen, Elizabeth II. She made him a Knight of the Garter, so he became 'Sir' Winston, and he was also honoured by the award of the Nobel prize for literature. A stroke just before his 80th birthday sapped some of his old energies, and in April 1955 he resigned as prime minister.

► Churchill shakes hands with his successor Sir Anthony Eden as he leaves office as prime minister in 1955.

■ Remembered by All ■

CHURCHILL REMAINED in the House of Commons as an MP until 1964, watching and commenting on many important events. In 1963 he was made an honorary US citizen by the United States Congress. He completed another book, *The History of the English-Speaking Peoples*.

He spent holidays in the South of France, and enjoyed oil painting (some of his pictures were shown at the Royal Academy in London) and pottering about the grounds of his country house, Chartwell, where over the years he had spent happy hours trying his hand at bricklaying.

▲ Churchill called painting his pastime, but he was accomplished as an artist.

▼ Admirers from all over the world sent greetings to Churchill. They knew no address was necessary.

His Last Farewells

In 1964, the year a new Labour government took power in Britain, Sir Winston Churchill said farewell to the House of Commons, the scene of so many dramatic and historic occasions. The veteran MP left with 'the unbounded admiration and gratitude' of Britain's law-makers.

On 24 January 1965 Churchill died in London – on the same date as his

▶ Sir Winston and Lady Clementine (Clemmie) in 1961. Two years later he was made an honorary citizen of the United States. President Kennedy called him 'the most honored and honorable man to walk the stage of history in the time in which we live'.

father, 70 years before. His state funeral brought the city, and the country, to a halt. Millions of people watched on television Churchill's last journey, from St Paul's Cathedral to the river Thames, and upstream to a modest grave in a quiet churchyard in Bladon, Oxfordshire.

STILL REMEMBERED

Churchill is remembered today as one of the greatest British leaders, and a world statesman. A statue of him stands facing the Houses of Parliament in London. Around the world, there are towns, rivers, streets and squares named after him. A college at Cambridge University bears his name and there are Churchill scholarships for young people.

In 2001 a new guided-missile destroyer, USS *Winston S Churchill*, joined the US Navy. It was the first US warship to carry the name of a foreigner and the first to have a British naval officer as a regular crew member. It marked the continuing friendship between the USA and Britain that Churchill had worked so hard to forge.

▲ Rather than be buried with other heroes in Westminster Abbey, Churchill chose to be buried with his parents and his brother Jack in a simple grave at Bladon near Blenheim Palace. His coffin was carried there by boat and train. In Westminster Abbey a stone slab bears the simple inscription: Remember Winston Churchill.

CHANGING WORLD

Much has changed since Churchill's time. Computers have changed the way we work. People have walked on the moon. The USSR is no more, and there are no Communist states in Europe. Germany, divided after World War II, is one country again and one of Britain's partners within the European Union. The Commonwealth now has 54 member-countries. Britain has changed too. As a reader and writer of history, Churchill knew well how the tide of events surges on.

▼ The USS *Winston S Churchill*, named in honour of the great world statesman. The ship's motto is: 'In war: resolution, In peace: good will.'

■ GLOSSARY ■

ABDICATE To give up the throne, as King Edward VIII did in 1936.

ADMIRALTY Government department in charge of Britain's navy.

ALLIES Countries on the same side in a war are allies, and belong to an alliance.

APPEASEMENT Trying to keep the peace by giving in to a threat. In 1938 Britain and France allowed Germany to bully weaker neighbours, in the vain hope of avoiding a war.

BIOGRAPHY Life story.

BLITZ Short for *blitzkrieg* (German for 'lightning war'), name given to the German bombing raids on Britain during World War II.

BOER South African farmers descended from Dutch settlers. Britain fought a war against the Boers from 1899 to 1902.

BOLSHEVIKS Group of Communists in Russia. Led by Lenin, they took power after the 1917 revolution, setting up the Soviet Union.

BY-ELECTION Election for Parliament, held when a Member of Parliament dies or resigns.

CARICATURE Drawing that exaggerates some familiar features of a person.

CAVALRY Soldiers who fight on horseback, becoming out of date by the time Churchill joined the army.

CHANCELLOR OF THE EXCHEQUER British government minister in charge of money matters and taxes.

CIVIL WAR Fighting within a country between rival groups.

COMMUNISM Revolutionary movement based on the ideas of German writer Karl Marx which sought to impose state control of all factories, transport, wealth and land.

CONSERVATIVE One of the three major political parties in Churchill's Britain, and the party he served as prime minister.

CORONATION Ceremony of crowning a king or queen, to show that they now hold the title.

D-DAY Code name for the Allied invasion of France during World War II (6 June 1944).

DICTATOR Ruler who is not controlled by a democratically elected parliament, and often rules harshly. Hitler and Stalin were both dictators, though with different ideas.

DIPHTHERIA Infectious throat disease, particularly dangerous to children.

DUKE Rank or title in British aristocracy. The title (Duke of Marlborough, for example) passes from father to eldest son.

EMPIRE A group of nations or states under one ruler. The British Empire included colonies (ruled by Britain) and self-governing dominions such as Canada and Australia.

FIGHTER PLANE Small fast aircraft that attack and shoot down enemy bombers. The RAF's Spitfire and Hurricane fighters played an heroic part in the Battle of Britain.

FINANCES Money matters.

FLOTILLA Fleet of small ships, of various kinds.

GENERAL ELECTION Election to Parliament in which people vote to choose all the MPs.

GUERRILLAS Irregular fighters, usually small groups who make fast-moving attacks or ambushes on a larger enemy army.

HOME SECRETARY British government minister in charge of law and order, justice and the police.

HUSSARS Cavalry soldiers, named after Hungary's national cavalry.

JUBILEE Special anniversary, especially a 50th.

LABOUR Political party which grew in power during Churchill's lifetime, and formed its first government under Ramsay Macdonald in 1924.

LANCERS Cavalry soldiers who rode into battle carrying a long spear or lance.

LIBERAL Political party to which Churchill belonged for a time. It rivalled the Conservatives in the 19th century.

MANOEUVRES Practices or 'war games' in which the army, navy and air force test new weapons and rehearse tactics they might use in battle.

MINISTER A senior member of the government, responsible for a department.

MP Stands for Member of Parliament, someone elected to represent a town or some other area (a constituency) in the House of Commons.

NANNY Woman employed to look after children in a wealthy household.

NATIONALISATION Taking control of private businesses (such as coal mines, steelworks, railways) by the government of a country.

NAZI Member of Germany's National Socialist Party, led by Adolf Hitler. Nazis believed Germans were superior to any other people.

OPPOSITION In Parliament, the smaller political party or group of parties which opposes and questions government actions.

PARLIAMENT An assembly of representatives who make laws for a country. Britain's Parliament has two parts or houses, the House of Commons and the House of Lords.

PNEUMONIA Serious illness affecting the lungs.

POLITICS The business of government – political parties are groups of people who share similar ideas about how a country should be run.

PRESIDENT An elected head of state, or leader of a country.

PRIME MINISTER The chief minister and head of the government in Britain, chosen by the party that wins a general election.

PROPAGANDA Government advertising, designed to show how right the government is. In war, both sides use propaganda to encourage their own people, and to scare or fool the other side's.

RATIONING Control of essential supplies such as food during war or some other emergency, with people allowed to buy only small amounts.

REVOLUTION Violent overthrow of one form of government and setting up a new one.

SCARLET FEVER Infectious fever, named after the reddish rash seen on people who catch it.

SLUMP Collapse in trade and business, leading to firms closing and workers losing their jobs.

STRIKE Refusal of workers to work, during a dispute with their employer or the government.

TANK Armoured military vehicle running on caterpillar tracks and heavily armed. An important weapon, first used in 1917.

UNITED NATIONS Organization set up by the victors after World War II to preserve world peace by settling arguments between nations without war.

VE DAY Popular name for the day on which World War II ended in Europe (8 May 1945), 'Victory in Europe Day'.

VICTORIAN Anything that happened during the reign of Queen Victoria (1837-1901).

PLACES TO VISIT

House of Commons/10 Downing Street
Westminster, London
Churchill's places of work, with his statue in Parliament Square.

Blenheim Palace
Oxfordshire
The great house of the Duke of Marlborough, where Churchill was born.

Chartwell
Kent
The country home in which Churchill and his family lived from 1924.

Cabinet War Rooms
The Mall/Horse Guards, London
Underground bomb-proof bunkers used by Churchill during the war and now restored to their wartime state, with maps and other reminders of what it was like to work there during the war.

Imperial War Museum
Lambeth, London
Has a wealth of information, in film, photos, documents and objects about both the World Wars of the 20th century.

INDEX